Carmen Sylva, John Eliot Bowen

Songs of toil

Carmen Sylva, John Eliot Bowen

Songs of toil

ISBN/EAN: 9783743334090

Hergestellt in Europa, USA, Kanada, Australien, Japan

Cover: Foto ©ninafisch / pixelio.de

Manufactured and distributed by brebook publishing software
(www.brebook.com)

Carmen Sylva, John Eliot Bowen

Songs of toil

SONGS OF TOIL

BY

CARMEN SYLVA, QUEEN OF RUMANIA

TRANSLATED BY

JOHN ELIOT BOWEN

With an Introductory Sketch

FOURTH EDITION

CONTENTS.

3

INTRODUCTORY SKETCH.

In writing of Carmen Sylva, Queen of Rumania, one does not know whether to call her poet-queen or queen-poet. Doubtless her royal position has had something to do with her fame as poet, and certainly her poetry has directed the world's eye to that far-off throne in southern Europe. She would not, then, be what she is, we are forced to conclude, were she not both poet and queen. Queens have always been interesting in literature, even if posing only as an inspiration. They have almost invariably been "fair women." Pictures and poems arise as we name them — Esther of Persia, Dido of Carthage, Cleopatra of Egypt, Mary of Scotland. The last is said even to have written poems herself; she certainly wrote a celebrated Latin hymn, but the poems — presumably not addressed to her cousin Elizabeth, else there would be no lack of fervor in them — do not find their place in literature. In general, royalty has inspired rather than produced literature. But with the present age this has changed. Applicable to monarchs as to men is the statement that "now-a-days every one writes books," and no truer in one case than in the other is the wicked end of the saying, " but

5

only fools publish them." The Queen of England publishes her journals; one of her daughters writes articles for the magazines; the King of Sweden prints sagas in verse; the Crown Prince of Austria publishes tales of travel and adventure; and even the Pope of Rome publishes to the world a collection of poems. But with all these the production of what may be kindly called literature, is pastime; to the Queen of Rumania, on the other hand, her literary work is life. How and why this is so may be learned from a brief glance at her career.

Like many of the heroines of fiction, Elizabeth, Princess of Wied and Queen of Rumania, was born of an ancient and honorable family. So far back as 1093, says Natalie Freiin von Stackelberg, in her life of Carmen Sylva,* the counts of Wied were a mighty race of rulers. Their possessions on the right and left banks of the Rhine stretched as far as Eifel and the Westerwald. Their most ancient residence was the castle of Upper-Altwied; afterward for generations the family lived in the castle of Lower-Altwied; and finally in the early part of the eighteenth century the castle of Neuwied was built, and in this the Princess Elizabeth was born. The town of Neuwied is situated in one of the most beautiful sections of the Rhine country. It is a short distance below Coblenz and on the same bank

---

* Aus Carmen Sylva's Leben. Von Natalie Freiin von Stadelberg.

as Ehrenbreitstein. The castle commands a most picturesque view of the cities and villages and mountain spurs that follow the winding course of the river.

With the fortunes of the family of Wied we are not specially concerned. The counts played their parts in the conflicts of the Middle Ages, in the Thirty Years' War, and in the Seven Years' War. In 1784 the countship of Wied was raised by Joseph II. to the dignity of a principality, but at the Congress of Vienna the semi-independence which the house had enjoyed, was taken away and the greater part of its possessions was placed under Prussian dominion.

It is of interest, however, to note that Elizabeth's family has been, to a considerable extent, a family of students, scholars, and even writers. The first distinguished scholar of the family was Maximilian, brother of Prince August and great-uncle of Elizabeth. His life was devoted to the study of natural history. During the first half of this century he travelled extensively in South and North America. His books descriptive of his journeys have been of value in their relation to the science of natural history, and his collection of specimens of mammalia, birds, fishes, reptiles, etc., has been purchased since his death by the American Museum of Natural History in Central Park, New York, where it is still exhibited under the name of "The Prince Maximilian of Wied Collection." Maximilian's sister, Louise, had special talents in music, painting and poetry.

Her "Songs of the Solitary," though perhaps over-pious, have a poetic quality. Prince Hermann, the father of Elizabeth, was a philosopher. The titles of his books and pamphlets are profound. For many years an invalid, he devoted himself assiduously to study and speculation, finding his sole recreation in the historical works of Mommsen, Häusser and Ranke, and in the occasional use of the brush, for which he had a natural talent. Elizabeth's mother, Maria, brought from the house of Nassau the qualities of heart that, in her child, were to find their complement in the qualities of mind bequeathed by the father. Of such stock and of such a union was Elizabeth, Princess of Wied, born.

The year of her birth was 1843, the month December, and the day 29. Her childhood was just what would be expected from her inheritances, and the method, manner and circumstances of life at Neuwied and Monrepos, the family's summer-house. Her bringing-up was superintended by her mother, acting under the advice of the Prince, her husband, and assisted by the same governess who had had charge of her own education. This governess had a rare fund of fairy tales and legends stored away in her memory, which were doubt-less the first stimulant applied to the young Elizabeth's imaginative powers. She was an original child. And yet in many respects she was like all children. She had a passion for dolls, which she called her children.

When she first met strangers her invariable question was, "Have you also children?" We learn in the poem entitled „Fiſcher," page —, which is tenderly and pathetically autobiographic, that this question of the child is still the question of the Queen. Stories of the little princess's generosity are told by Natalie von Stackelberg, to whom I must acknowledge my indebtedness for all anecdotes not otherwise credited. When the merest child she was filled with compassion for the poor. One day her mother gave her a quantity of new woolen cloth, greatly to Elizabeth's delight, "for now," she said, "I can give all my dresses to the poor." "But," said the mother, "would it not be better to give the cloth to the poor, to whom your white dresses would be of little use?" The princess, who was by no means a goody-goody child, and had a will of her own, comprehended, nevertheless, her mother's question, and with her little brother at once set forth to carry the cloth to a poor woman.

Many of the stories of Elizabeth's youthful years have become household tales, and scarcely need to be told again. All who know anything of her childhood will remember how she played truant, not by staying away from school, but by going to school one day. She had always, during the beautiful summer-days at Monrepos, had a great desire to attend school with the village children. Permission had been denied her until one morning she rushed in upon her mother, who was

absorbed in household duties, and begged to be allowed
to go to school with the farm children. Without com-
prehending the question the mother nodded her con-
sent, and away ran the little princess. She arrived at
the school while the singing lesson was in progress and
at once took her place beside the other children, greatly
to the satisfaction of the school-master, who was
flattered by her presence. He had no mark of reproof
for her when she raised her voice to such a pitch as to
drown the voices of all the other children. Not so,
however, with the child who stood next to her, and who
thought it unbecoming to sing so loud. This youngster
clapped her hand over the princess's mouth by way of
rebuke, and to show that the other children, if they did
not have equal voices, had at least equal rights. In the
meantime the absence of the princess had been noticed
at the palace, and after a vain search the servants were
put on the right track and found and carried the child
home in disgrace. This story ought to end here; for
we are sorry to learn that the democratic enthusiasm of
the child was punished by imprisonment for the re-
mainder of the day.

Elizabeth's interest in poetry was excited at an ex-
tremely early age. There is no doubt but that she felt
the influence of the poets with whom, in company with
her parents, she frequently came in contact. During a
brief residence in Bonn they were visited almost daily
by Ernst Moritz Arndt, the poet, who, with the eight-

year-old princess on his knee, would recite his patriotic poems till the child's cheek flushed and her heart beat with excitement. Among their other frequent visitors were Lessing, Bunsen, Neukomm and others distinguished in literature. But not only was she privileged to hear poetry; she was compelled to learn it. Every Sunday morning she and her little brothers were obliged to recite poems to their father and mother. By the time the princess was nine years old, she could commit a poem of almost any length to memory, provided only it were not in the Alexandrine meter, which was to her an abomination. At this time also she began to write occasional verses herself. When scarcely fourteen she had plotted dramas and dreadful tragedies. The more horrible these latter were, the better she liked them. Though she read early and late only the most beautiful poems, her fantasy produced only the most terrible ideas. This constant contrast in absorption and production had its effect upon her moods, which were alternately gay and melancholy. "I cannot help myself," she was wont to confess mentally; "I cannot be gentle; I must rage. I would thank these mortals from the bottom of my heart, if they only had patience with me. It would not be so bad if I could but open the safety-valve and let the poetry come." When, later in life, there was cause for the deepest woe and melancholy, this safety-valve opened of itself.

At fifteen years of age Elizabeth settled down to

study in earnest. Her governess was replaced by a tutor, who was an excellent English scholar. All the lessons were conducted in English. She studied English history, arithmetic and geometry, and translated into English, Italian and Latin, reading in the latter Horace, Ovid and a part of Cicero. She had lessons in natural philosophy from the father of an intimate friend. A Parisienne instructed her in French, and read with her in the evening the chronicles and memoirs of Froissart, Joinville, St. Simon and others, and the dramas of Molière, Racine and Corneille. To her mother she read aloud the German classics and Schiller's "Thirty-Years' War." Lessing's „Nathan der Weise" she read to her again and again. In one summer she read Becker's History of the World from first page to last, and did the same with Gibbon's history. She read daily three newspapers, and devoted herself to politics. She studied with interest and enthusiasm, but as she said herself, she would throw history or grammar, for which she had a passion, into the corner if she could put her hand upon a tale or legend. She came upon Elizabeth Wetherell's "The Wide, Wide World," and read it time after time with devouring interest. Like many another school-girl, she buried the book under her Ovid translations, and stole from Duty in order that she might give to Pleasure. No one will begrudge her the mild excitement when he learns that until her nineteenth year she was never allowed to look into a novel of any kind. Even then she was only permitted to read "Ivanhoe" and Freytag's „Soll und Haben" in the evening after her cup of tea. This was a rather serious life for a girl of Elizabeth's temperament, but fortunately she was able to find poetic diversion even in the midst of such tasks. She found it in the life at Monrepos. This beautiful summer home is high upon one of the hills composing the range of the Westerwald Mountains. It commands a more extensive view than the castle at Neuwied, and at the same time it includes within its horizon all the points of beauty that can be seen from the castle in the town, upon which it looks down. The glory of Monrepos lies in the forest that stretches away from it in mile after mile of grateful shade. "Here the princess Elizabeth was in her element," says her biographer; "here were forest and freedom." She roamed careless and gay, with Nature for her only companion. She listened to the voices of Nature, to the singing of the birds, to the rustling of the leaves, to the rippling of the Wiedbach, and to the moaning of the tree-tops; and she whispered the secrets of her heart to her voiceful and sympathetic companion. She whispered in song, the first songs of a young poet-life. She roamed and sang, and the people called her the Forest-Rose Princess. From her sixteenth year she began to copy her poems regularly in a book, whose existence she confessed to no one. She wrote simply and naturally, with never a rule to follow but the notes of a bird or the beatings of her heart. Until she was thirty years old she knew absolutely nothing of the art of poetical composition.

She was not happy away from her forest home. When seventeen, she made a visit to Berlin, and she filled her journal with home-sick verses and songs of melancholy. She longed for the breath of the forest and the sight of the Rhine. But this visit is remembered less for these youthful verses than for an accident or incident that befell the Princess. It was nothing serious, nothing more than falling down the stairs of the palace into the arms of the prince who was one day to become her husband. The story seems to be founded only on a kind of gossipy tradition, bu there is a flavor of romance about it that has led the superstitious, viewing the incident from this side of the marriage, to believe that the union was fated to occur from the day Elizabeth fell into the arms of Prince Charles of Hohenzollern on the palace stair.

In February of 1862, when the princess was eighteen years old, her younger brother, Prince Otto, died, after a long period of invalidism. The parents were grateful that their son's suffering was at an end, but the death was a great sorrow to Elizabeth. The palace seemed hollow and deserted, and even when she sought the mountain heights she could not get above the heaviness of her heart. For a few months she held a little school among some poor children, and found diversion in her zeal as teacher. To them she devoted three hours a day; she read to her invalid father another three hours; and for four or five hours she devoted herself to the piano. But when the winter came on, Prince Hermann's state of health required a change of climate. They went to Baden-Baden, and for a time Elizabeth enjoyed the gayeties of life; but while there she received the news of the death of her dearest friend, Marie von Bibra. This death set the sorrowing muse to work again, and many a mourning song was the result. In the autumn of 1863, however, the sorrow was again dispelled by the pleasures of travel. She was invited to accompany the Grand Duchess Helene of Russia, a relative of her mother's, in a visit to Switzerland. So happy was their life together at Ouchy, on Lake Geneva, that the Grand Duchess invited the young Princess to return to St. Petersburg with her. There she studied the Russian language, read, and took music lessons, first of Rubinstein, and later of Clara Schumann. While on this visit, her father died after years of suffering. But Elizabeth, who was just recovering from a severe illness contracted in St. Petersburg, did not return at once to Neuwied. In June of 1864, however, she was with her mother again in Monrepos, which now became their home for both winter and summer.

From 1864 until 1868, Elizabeth's life was uneventful except for several journeys in her own country, trips to

Paris and Sweden, and an extended visit in Italy. It was while in Naples that the Princess came to the conclusion, as the natural result of her studies and sympathies, that she was by nature fitted and by heart inclined to become a teacher. She was then twenty-four years old. She wrote to her mother that she was determined, if she did not marry, to prepare for the teacher's examination. She was willing, however, patiently to bide her time. But she did not tarry that suitors might make their bows before her. She would have none of them. One day some friends who were discussing matrimonial projects with her, said they would like to see her on a throne. "The only throne that would allure me," she jokingly replied, "would be the Rumanian; for there would still be a chance there to accomplish something." In the light of subsequent facts this joke about a throne that did not then exist must be considered little less than marvellous, and it is not only the superstitious who wag their heads when they come to this point of the story of Carmen Sylva's life, and mutter their proverbs about true words and jests.

Rumania was only a principality subject to the Sublime Porte, when in 1866 Prince Charles of Hohenzollern was placed at the head of the state, with the title of Prince Charles I. of Rumania. He had distinguished himself in the Austro-Prussian war, that grew out of the Schleswig-Holstein conflict; and even before that General von Moltke had said, "The young Prince of Hohenzollern is destined to play a rôle in life and to let himself be heard from." He had not been long in Rumania when he made up his mind that the country needed a princess as much as it had needed a prince, and as quickly he made up his mind that ne would offer his heart to Elizabeth of Wied, whom he remembered to have met in Berlin, and with whom his sister had kept up an active correspondence. The Prince confessed the desire of his heart to Elizabeth's mother, who undertook to assist him in his suit, or rather, in true German fashion, to conduct it for him. A rendezvous that should appear accidental was arranged at Cologne, and there, in October of 1869, Prince Charles and Princess Elizabeth met, fell in love, and became engaged all in the space of an afternoon. The engagement was a short one of necessity, and on the 15th of November the marriage was celebrated in Neuwied with such pomp and circumstance as the quiet Rhenish town had never seen before. But it was all as nothing compared with the splendor of the reception in Rumania, and of the marriage ceremony according to the rites of the Greek Church.

After her marriage, Elizabeth devoted herself at once to the study of the institutions of the country and of the language of the people, which, being a Latin and not a Slavic language, was easily acquired by her in consequence of her knowledge both of Latin and

Italian. In September of 1870, the Princess became the mother of a daughter. For four years only did this child live, but those four years were the happiest Elizabeth had known since her own childhood. The full, warm love of her nature she bestowed upon her little Marie. The child was one of hundreds of children to succumb to what seemed a plague of diphtheria, typhoid and scarlet fevers, which raged in Bucharest during the winter of 1873 and 1874. Until April Marie withstood the diseases, but then scarlet fever, followed by diphtheria attacked her, and the slender body of the child had to yield. The deathbed scene was woefully pathetic. The mother watched hopeless and helpless above Marie till the last. The little one in her delirium started from her trundle-bed and would not lie down. "Oh, no, no!" she said in terror, "if I lie down I shall fall asleep and never wake up any more." And again she exclaimed: "I want to go to Sinaia, and drink of the water of Pelesch." But when a glass was reached out to her, she shook her head and said, in English, "All is finished," and shortly after passed away in her English nurse's arms. The mother stood there immovable, without a tear and without a complaint; she said, simply and reverently, "The good Lord loved my child more than I, and has taken her to him. I thank God he gave her to me."

This loss was to Elizabeth like the end of life. She had, as we have seen, met death before. First her brother, then her father, and one friend and relative after another had been taken from her. Her sorrow in each case was keen; but now it was dull and heavy, and harder and enduring. It permeated her life; and yet she did not wholly give up to it. It broadened her sympathies and increased her benevolences, and, indeed, widened the scope of her life, and made her the "little mother" of her people. To them she had devoted herself from the first. She had found that the jesting words of her maidenhood were true indeed: here, in Rumania, there was still a chance to accomplish something. Her first work had been for the school-children. A poor-union was established to provide proper books for the education of the children. The Princess found that there were absolutely no school-books or popular works in the Rumanian language, and she set about translating at once the best French books for children. Her object was less to interest the young than to develop a strong national character, which she well knew could not exist without the basis of language. In other ways, too, she sought to strengthen Rumanian nationality. She encouraged the use of the national costume, and made the wearing of it obligatory at the public charity balls in Bucharest. She established a school of embroidery, which is one of the national industries, and a union called "Concordia," whose purpose is to further the development of all national industries. She founded also an asylum for orphans and waifs, in which between four and five hundred girls from five to twenty years of age are housed and educated in the practical affairs of life. We are told that the reputation of this home is so exceptional and wide-spread that the young men of Rumania think themselves lucky if they can choose a wife from among the industrious girls in the " Asyle Hélène." To sum up in the words of Miss Zimmern,* " She founded schools, hospitals, soup-kitchens, convalescent homes, cooking-schools, and *crèches;* she encouraged popular lectures; she inculcated respect for sanitary laws, most needful in an eastern land; she founded art galleries and art schools." Some of her charitable enterprises, not here enumerated, were described to me in a recent letter from the Queen's private secretary, Mr. Robert Scheffer, to whom I am indebted for many suggestions and kindnesses. Concluding his description, he says: " But as the Queen does not like her charitable works to be known, I shall only add that the quantity of good done by her Majesty in private is incalculable, and not one-tenth of it is known by the public."

All this work, which she had begun while " Itty," as her little daughter was endearingly called, was still alive, the childless mother found a sweet solace in the days of her great sorrow. A still greater comfort, however, was found in an appeal to that talent which had been hers from childhood, but which had never been

---

* The Century Magazine, August, 1884.

cultivated. No one dreamed that the Princess Elizabeth was a poet. But one day a native poet named Alexandri called upon her in Bucharest, and she said to him : " I would like to make a confession to you, but I have not the courage for it." After a long silence, however, and amid many blushes, she added : " I, too, make verses." At Alexandri's request she produced some of her songs, and the poet was warm in his praise of them. He urged her to continue writing, and indited many poems to her himself, which she translated from the Rumanian tongue into German. While at work upon these translations, she wrote :

" The greatest possible change has come over my poet-life. I had no idea that poetizing is an art, or that one must learn how to be a poet. I had supposed that to learn to make poems would be like a man teaching a bird to sing. Verses and rhymes flowed from my pen more easily than prose. I feared, as soon as I attempted to bind myself to rules and methods, I should forfeit my talent as punishment of my empty conceit. In the terrible pain of the spring of 1874, songs were no longer a relief. Only the strain of exhausting toil could deaden it. And so I took to translating."

She applied herself diligently to this work, and said soon after that she had learned more by translating than in any other way. She showed her work to another poet of local fame, whose advice and assistance she received. In the following summer, with her mother, she paid a visit to England, and spent two days with Max Müller at Oxford. She had with her a little book in the form of a missal, which she had prepared for her mother, and which she called "My Journey through the World: a collection of Rhymes and Verses, dedicated to the Mother Heart." The book contained the poems that she had composed from her sixteenth to her thirtieth year. Scarcely one of these was known to her mother. Charles Kingsley was present when she surprised her mother with the gift. Elizabeth showed to them the four lines in which she prayed God to preserve her child from unhappiness, want, and sin; and as she pronounced the last line: „Du weißt es: Ich habe nur Eines," Kingsley's eyes filled with tears, and the mother wept for joy and pain.

In January, 1875, Elizabeth wrote: "I am not translating at all now, because I write so much myself." Her poetic activity was at its height when she was visiting Sinaia. This beautiful region was to Bucharest what Monrepos had been to Neuwied. Here again she found freedom and the forest. The beautiful stream of Pelesch dances down the rough side of the mountains and winds into the valley of Sinaia. It is shaded by primeval forests in which the nightingales sing and the wild-flowers bloom. There the sad mother-heart found rest even while her mind was inspired to activity. In this region of beautiful wildness she laid the corner-stone of her summer-house in August of 1875, and the dancing stream, for whose water her child called in its last delirium, gave its name to the castle whose towers rise among the trees of the forest. The princess watched the progress of the structure with the greatest possible interest, and with no little sympathy for the workmen whose polyglot of tongues — no less than twelve in number — made the silences about the forest and the quarries ring with strange sounds. Had she not watched the toilers in the quarry near by, from which all the material for the castle was taken, she probabably would never have written the touching song of „Steinſchneider," page 142.

It was at the end of this summer that Elizabeth wrote the libretto for an operetta performed during the following winter in Bucharest. The work was a poetical adaptation of an old Rumanian legend.

When the princess had been working at her poetry zealously for more than two years, at such times and hours as freedom from official life permitted, and just at the time when she had sufficient material to lead her to think of publishing her work to the world, the Turko-Russian war broke out, and Rumania became the battle-ground of a terrible conflict. That was not a time for poetry, except of the heroic order. The poetry of words was forgotten in the poetry of deeds. Prince Charles of necessity took Russia's side, and became a gallant leader against the Turkish crescent. Princess Elizabeth followed the army, and sought to temper the misery of the battle-field. She was the Florence Nightingale of the war. Her people called her "the mother of the wounded." Childless, she was always a mother.

She moved from bed to bed in the hospitals, and spoke words of comfort, nay almost of healing. She was worshipped by every sufferer. At the close of the war a marble statue was raised to her by the wives of the officers of the Rumanian army as a memorial of the merciful part played by her on the battle-field. Following the war there was a rearrangement of boundary and territory between Russia and Rumania, which was ratified by the treaty of Berlin, which, at the same time. recognized the independence of Rumania as a kingdom, though providing that certain conditions should be fulfilled. These were carried out, and in March, 1881, Prince Charles issued his royal proclamation. On the 22d of May he was crowned with a diadem made from cannon captured at Plevna, where he distinguished himself, as did his people, for bravery. At the same time a golden crown was placed upon the head of "the mother of the wounded." The ceremony was carried out with true royal magnificence, and the day and night were given up to festivities and rejoicing.

It is only since the end of the Turko-Russian war that the Queen, as we must now call her, has appeared in literature. It was in 1880 that the first book was published, bearing on its title-page the name "Carmen Sylva"—an appropriate pen-name for one who loves the song and the forest as Elizabeth always has. This first book consists of translations into German of the Rumanian poems of Alexandri and others. At this same time she wrote a French comedy for a company in Bucharest, and a number of aphorisms in French, which were afterwards published in Paris under the title of " Pensées d'une Reine." * In 1881 the queen published her first book of original poems. The book is entitled „Stürme" and contains four poems: „Sappho," „Hammerstein," „Ueber den Wassern," and „Schiffbruch." I cannot go into a criticism of these poems, which are of varying merit. Both Miss Zimmern † and Professor Boyesen ‡ agree that „Sappho" is the best of the four. Of this Professor Boyesen says : —

"Miss Zimmern has anticipated me in saying that " Sappho," the principal poem in this volume, is quite un-Greek. It is, in fact, both in form and conception, as Germanic as possible. It has none of the bright and unconscious sensuousness and heedless grace of Greek song. The fateful dream of Laïs, the daughter of Sappho, with which the poem opens, bears some resemblance to the dream of Chriemhild in the first canto of the " Niebelungen Lay," although butterflies are substituted for eagles. But apart from the moral anachronism which is implied in the domestic virtues and Teutonic conscientiousness of the Lesbian poetess, there is much to admire. As a mere woman, without reference to age or nationality, Sappho is strongly and vividly delineated, and the songs which she sings,

---

* That this work has a high standing in France may be judged from the fact that the French Academy, on April 25, 1888, voted to offer its author a medal of honor, devoting to this purpose a part of the accrued interest of the prize-fund established by Mrs. Vincengo Botta, of New York, for literary works composed by women.

† The Century Magazine, August, 1884.

‡ The Independent, November 24, 1887.

though they have neither the Sapphic meter nor spirit, are lyrical
gems which we could ill afford to miss. Thus the charming little
lay : „Wenn tobt ich werbe fein," in the third canto, has an "un-
premeditated art" which none but true singers attain. It expires
like a sigh in the air, and is as eloquent of the emotion which
prompted it. The hexameter in "Sappho" is handled with much
skill ; but the perpetually occurring alliteration, to my mind, inter-
feres with its melodious effect. As a metrical device alliteration is of
Germanic origin, and seems alien to the spirit of Greek poetry.
There is also a certain exasperating monotony in the constantly re-
peated initial letters, which gives an air of artificiality even to the
noblest verse."

In 1882 appeared „Die Hexe," a collection of poems
inspired by Carl Cauer's statue of " The Witch." Of
this book Miss Zimmern says : —

" This work is very characteristic of the Queen's writings, in that
she is apt to write too fast, so that excellent fundamental ideas are
made abortive by inadequate execution. She does not observe the
Horation maxim ; the impetuosity that is a part of her character is
reflected in her work. She lacks patience. This fault is really to be
deplored, and the more that the Queen has genuine poetical gifts, a
fine fancy, a musical ear, fire, and grace. But her facility consti-
tutes her weakness. Had she not been a royal author, had she had
to do battle with the exigencies, caprices, uncertainties of publishers
and editors, she would have received just that schooling which she
lacks, and which hinders her from being a great poet, and confines
her within the ranks of minor singers."

I cannot find the evidences of haste that appear
to Miss Zimmern. The portions of „Die Hexe" that
might have been hurriedly done are those written in an
unrhymed trochaic tetrameter, but even these show no

carelessness in construction. And there are poems in the work which are as good in point of technique as anything the Queen has done. It is, moreover, hardly fair to charge with violation of the Horatian maxim one who kept the secret of her compositions to herself from her sixteenth to her thirtieth year, and only began to publish when she was nearly forty.

The next poetical work of Carmen Sylva's that was published is entitled „Jehovah." It describes the wanderings of Ahasuerus in search of God. His journey begins with the scoffing assertion, „Es ist kein Gott!" and ends with the acknowledgment, „Gott ist ewig Werden." The poem tells its story with force and fervor. "It would be vain," says Professor Boyesen, "to deny the exalted beauty and dignity of the verse in which the wrestlings of Ahasuerus with the infinite are depicted." The Queen's next volume of verse made its appearance in 1883, under the title of „Meine Ruh." This is a collection of lyrics and songs — the kind of verse that shows Carmen Sylva to the best advantage. This was apparent even in „Sappho," the most beautiful parts of which are the songs, introduced in much the same way and to the same purpose as the interludes are introduced by Tennyson in the "Princess." The first poem of „Meine Ruh" is called „Carmen" and the last, „Sylva." Between these boundaries the Queen has poured out her heart and made her appeals to and from nature, and written down her pretty conceits and the epigrams in which she delights. The first edition of „Meine Ruh" was quickly exhausted, and I have been unable to obtain a copy, much to my regret, as it contained the first series of „Handwerkerlieder" — "Songs of Toil." These were withheld by the Queen from the second edition in order that she might improve and enlarge the series, which has now been concluded, and comprises the poems originally published in „Meine Ruh," and those now first gathered in this volume. The Queen will publish the entire collection in a volume by itself, I am informed, some time during the coming winter.

To a book of poems published in 1884 Carmen Sylva gave her whole heart; for this one is entitled „Mein Rhein!" Here she writes of the places she loves most, the spots dear to her Jugendzeit. „Bingen," „Lorelei," „Die Mosel," „Monrepos," „Altwied," are some of the titles of the thirty songs that make up this book. The songs are as sweet and simple as the twenty etchings that adorn the volume are beautiful. One more volume of poems has followed this. It is entitled „Mein Buch," and contains a collection of poems upon Egypt. I have not been able to secure the volume, and cannot speak of its merits.

Of the Queen's recent prose works I have space to give little more than the titles. They comprise: „Leidens Erdengang" (1882), a collection of Rumanian legends; „Aus Carmen Sylva's Königreich" (1883), also a collection of tales, which were revised in a new edition published last year; „Ein Gebet" (1883), a story; „Aus Zwei Welten" (1885), a novel; „Aftra" (1886), a novel; „Es Klopft" (1887), a story; and „Feldpoft" (1887), a novel. In the composition of „Aus Zwei Welten," „Aftra," and „Feldpoft" as well as of a collection of tales called „In der Irre" the Queen had the collaboration of the Frau Dr. Kremnitz. In August of 1887 the Queen translated a novel by Pierre Loti in the space of fourteen days, and published the book under the title of „Islandfifdjer." During this period of marvellous literary activity the Queen also revised and brought out a new edition of her "Les Pensées d'une Reine." She has had the satisfaction of seeing many of her songs set to music by Bungert, Reinecke, and other composers. Some are now in preparation by Madame Augusta Holmès and Charles Gounod; and Bungert, I am informed, is to set the „Handwerferlieder" to music. It is now necessary that I speak in detail of these „Handwerferlieder" or "Songs of Toil," to which I have several times alluded.

The "Songs of Toil," which give this volume its name, have never been published in Germany or Rumania. Seventeen of these songs, in German and in English, were first published in *The Independent* of New York, in November, 1887. Six others were published in the same journal in July of the present year. The rest appear now for the first time. Early in the summer

of 1887 I wrote to Carmen Sylva, in my capacity of edi·
tor of the poetical department of *The Independent*,
asking her to contribute to the columns of which I had
charge. I received in reply seventeen "songs," together
with the following note from the Queen's secretary:

CASTEL PELESCH, August 21st, 1887.

Secretariat de S. M. La Reine de Roumanie.

EDITOR OF THE INDEPENDENT:

Sir:— In answer to your honored of the 16th past, Her Majesty
the Queen, breaking for once her rule of never giving any of her
productions to a periodical, charges me to send you the second
series of „Handwerkerlieder," the first of which was published in
Carman Sylva's „Meine Ruh." The inclosed seventeen songs,
being of quite recent date, have not yet appeared in print, and Her
Majesty leaves it to your choice to publish them all or to make a
selection of those most adapted to the American public. In case the
peculiar and essentially German character of the poems should render
a satisfactory translation in verse difficult, Her Majesty thinks it
would suffice to give the German original, adding to it a good translation in prose. As to the offered *honorarium*, Her Majesty is
pleased to accept it as a contribution to the sums produced by the
sale of her other works, which form a special fund for needy authors;
you will please send the money to me. I beg also that you will give
me immediate notice on receipt of the manuscript, and I am, sir,

Your obedient servant,

ROBERT SCHEFFER,

Private Secretary to Her Majesty the Queen of Rumania.

After these poems had been published, the Queen
herself wrote me the following note:

Sir : — Your translations of my songs are so very beautiful that I was quite surprised in reading them. There are very few little things you have perhaps misunderstood, but they are scarcely worth while talking of when it is all so very good. As I have translated a good deal myself, I know the difficulties very well, and I admire your work in consequence. I am very happy to be brought in so beautiful a clothing before your American public, and I thank you kindly for all the pains you have taken.

ELIZABETH.

With this note the Queen sent me „Juli," page 62, and „Scheerenschleiferlied," page 38, and subsequently her secretary forwarded to me the twelve additional songs which are included in this volume.

It is fortunate that the American public should first know the Queen as a poet through these „Handwerker-lieder ;" for they are at once the index of her character and the illustration of her genius. I say genius, for certainly the chief attribute of genius is not wanting — originality. The „Handwerkerlieder" in conception and expression are original. It is true that in some of them, in the „Bäckerlied," page 92, and in „Der Geigen-macher," page 138, for example, there is a suggestion of Heine; but this is so slight that we may say that the Queen's songs are distinctively her own. And they are the index of her character. No one can read these songs and not know the Queen. She said herself, in one of her letters quoted by her biographer: " The pictures of my fantasy are seldom gay — they never were." Her life has been a sad one, and most of these

songs are sung in a minor key. But it is not a selfish
sadness that the poems reveal. On the contrary, her
boundless sympathy for the poor is the most striking
disclosure of these " Songs of Toil." It is as special as
it is comprehensive. In each case does she seem to have
entered into the life, made up of trials, hope, pride, am-
bition, discouragement, sorrow, or joy of the one whose
song she is singing. No proud queen ever showed such
touch of sympathy. She has the soul to feel and the
gift to sing. Into the lives of others she pours her own
heart-beats. How admirably in the „Schifferlied," page
68, has she contrasted the two phases of the boatman's
life, whose home is on the Danube. We see him one day
sailing merrily down with the current, the picture of in-
dolent ease and joy; and the next day we see him toiling
along the sandy shore, towing his boat to the upper
stream, his task severe, but his progress sure. Again,
one is at a loss to fancy how so disagreeable a subject
as the „Metzger" could have been treated better than
in the grimly humorous way in which the Queen has
set forth the „Metzgerlied," page 40. In „Der Sä=
mann," page 64, what a vivid glimpse of the farmer
sowing his seed do the words „Zwei Schritte dann die
Handvoll" present! Again there is genius in the co-
quetry of the mill-stream; the pathos of the „Zimmer=
mannslied," page 42, is as simple as it is sweet; „Beim
Füttern" page 52, and „Beim Molken," page 56, carry
the odor of clover with them; and so on through the

list we find that each has a charm or a piquancy of its own, until we come to the „Steinschneider,“ page 142, where we are forced to believe that the question of the concluding lines, with its inevitable answer "No!" applies to the toiling poor of whatever trade or calling.

In speaking of the „Handwerkerlieder,“ I must not overlook their mechanism. The measures are chosen with an appreciation that is little short of inspiration. For example, wherever the trade of a songster is associated with any kind of noise or motion, we have both sound and motion reproduced in the meter; this onomatopœia is especially noticeable in the „Müllerlied,“ page 48; the „Töpferlied“ page 98; „Papiermacher,“ page 46; „Beim Spinnen,“ page 80; and „Der Bläser,“ page 130. The Queen has an excellent musical ear; the numerous feminine endings and the double rhymes are sufficient proof of this. One is even inclined to admit that her variation of the sonnet form is felicitous, as it appears in „Der Farbenreiber,“ page 88; „Der Landbriefträger,“ page 116; and „Der Sämann,“ page 64. This substitution for the iambic pentameter of an iambic hexameter with extra syllables at the end of the third and sixth foot is a musical device of which the Hungarian poet Lenau has availed himself in at least one notable instance. It is quite possible that his poem, „Der Herbstabend,“ may be a favorite with the Queen.

In concluding this sketch of Carmen Sylva's life and

work, and in presenting the translations of her „𝔖𝔞𝔫𝔟𝔴𝔢𝔯𝔨𝔢𝔯𝔩𝔦𝔢𝔟𝔢𝔯," I must urge that her graceful style is not to be judged by whatever harshness there may be in the English versions. Read the original, those who can; the translation, those who must; read, and you will accept the statement of the venerable poet Whittier, that the Queen of Rumania is "crowned not alone with a diadem and title, but with the laurel-wreaths of poetic genius."

J. E. B.

New York, August, 1888.

SONGS OF TOIL.

SONGS OF TOIL.

THE SCISSORS-GRINDER'S SONG.

FETCH on your scissors, your slender blade —
　　To make them brilliant and sharp's my trade;
To every door-step my grindstone comes,
And on and ever it strolls and hums.

I and my grindstone, we wander by,
And no one asks me from whence come I;
How poor I am, no one cares to know,
None care to hear of my spirit's woe.

I'm ground by sorrow both day and night,
And yet I never am polished bright;
I'm ground by hunger, and though it pales
The face, to sharpen the wit it fails.

Handwerkerlieder.

Scheerenschleiferlied.

Bringt her die Scheeren, die Klingen fein,
   Ich mach' sie glänzend und scharf und rein;
Es harrt mein Rädchen vor jeder Thür,
Und schnurrt und wandert so für und für.

Ich und mein Rädchen, wir geh'n vorbei;
Es fragt mich Keiner, woher ich sei;
Will Keiner wissen wie arm ich bin,
Will Keiner hören wie weh mein Sinn.

Mich schleift die Sorge bei Tag und Nacht,
Und hat mich dennoch nicht fein gemacht;
Mich schleift der Hunger, und macht doch nicht
Den Witz mir schärfer ein blank Gesicht.

Mich schleift die Reue, und läßt mir doch
Das Herze schartig und rostig noch.
Das Rad ist emsig und rauh der Stein —
Bringt her die Klingen — ich mach' sie fein?

38

I'm ground by grief, but the work is ill,

For notched and rusty my heart is, still.

The wheel is whirling, the stone has grit —

Fetch on your steel — shall I sharpen it?

Metzgerlied.

Ich bin ein Henker, ich schwinge das Beil,
  Und wen ich treffe, wird nicht mehr heil;
Und wen ich binde kann nicht mehr geh'n;
Weß Kopf ich fasse, kann nimmer steh'n.

Ich bin ein Doktor, drum kommt zu mir!
Ich heile jedes Gebrechen hier;
Die Lebensmüdigkeit geht fürbaß
Mit einem einzigen Aderlaß.

Ich bin ein Wirth und mein Wein ist roth,
Und mit der Kreide hat's keine Noth;
Vor meiner Schenke geht nicht vorbei,
Die Ruh' ist sicher, die Zeche frei!

40

THE BUTCHER'S SONG.

I AM a headsman, the ax I swing,
   And if I strike that ends the thing;
And what I tie up cannot get loose —
The head I grapple can't slip the noose.

I am a doctor, so come to me;
Here heal I every infirmity;
The hypochondria is cured for good
By only a single letting of blood.

I am a landlord, my wine is red;
I chalk no slate when a man is fed;
Don't pass the inn that belongs to me;
The rest is certain; the score is free!

41

Zimmermannslied.

Mir ging es gut, so nach und nach;
    Die Kinder wurden groß:
Mein eigen Haus war unter Dach —
    So schön war mir kein Schloß!
Und: „Vater!" sagt sie, „Weißt Du noch?
    Einst gab es trocken Brod!
Jetzt zieh'n ins eigne Haus wir doch!"—
    Die Mutter, die ist todt!

Der Schreiner hat ihr Haus gebaut,
    Und nicht der Zimmermann;
Statt meiner hat der Pfarrer laut
    Den Segensspruch gethan.
Mit Feiersang und Glockenklang,
    Und Blumen blau und roth,
Statt Gläserklang das Herz mir sprang; —
    Die Mutter, die ist todt!

MY lot grew lighter day by day;
  The children grew apace;
I built a little house last May —
  No palace like that place.
And — "Father," said she, "sure you know
  That once we ate dry bread?
Into our own house now we go!"—
  The Mother, she is dead!

Her house the undertaker made,
  And not the carpenter;
My grace unsaid, the pastor prayed
  In loud tones over her.
The day that's spent with merriment,
  'Mid blossoms blue and red,
No music lent — my heart was rent!—
  The mother, she is dead.

Wir hatten's doch so weit gebracht,
 Wir altes Vogelpaar!
Wer hat an's Sterben auch gedacht,
 Als man beisammen war!
Verrammelt sind die Fenster dicht —
 Damit hat's keine Noth —
Verkauft das Haus! Ich mag es nicht —
 Die Mutter, die ist todt!

We pulled together many a year;
  Like old bird-mates were we;
But who e'er thinks of dying here
  While both together be?
Fast barred is every window-blind —
  I care not what is said;
Yes, sell the house! I do not mind —
  The mother, she is dead!

Papiermacher.

Die alten Lappen mir zugeführt!
  Die schmutz'gen Lumpen hineingerührt —

Zum Brei, zum Brei, wie das Weltgericht!
Zum Brei, zum Brei, wie ein lang Gedicht!

Dann kommt es schneeig und glatt heraus,
Aus Rollen und Walzen und Radgebraus,

Zu großen Herrn, mit der Fräulein Zier;
Für kleine Dichter, zum Nachtgeschmier;

Zu Zeitungsschreibern mit Posteshauch;
Für Liebesbriefchen mit Schmeichelrauch;

Und zu Romanen, d'rin schlecht erzählt,
Wie sich die Menschheit so weiter quält,

Auf gleichen Fetzen, in den dereinst
Die Thränen strömten, um die du weinst!

46

THE PAPER-MAKER.

THOSE pieces of rags be quick and bring!
 The dirty old shreds are just the thing —

For pulp, for pulp to record life's wrong,
For pulp, for pulp for a poet's song.

It comes out smooth and glossy and thin,
From rollers and wheels and cylinders' din,

For lords and ladies their notes to indite;
For petty poets, who scrawl by night,

And newspaper scribblers who bluster and blow;
For little love-letters where compliments grow;

And stories in which the afflictions of men
Are wretchedly told by an unskilled pen

On just such rags as once wiped away
The tears whereat thou weepest to-day!

Müllerlied.

Sowie vom Wasser
   Das Mühlrad geht,
So wird vom Liebchen
   Mein Sinn gedreht.

Es kost, es streichelt,
   Es schilt und sprüht,
Und lacht und wendet
   Mir mein Gemüth.

Wie steif ich wehre,
   Sie spricht so schnell;
Und brummend wendet
   Sich ihr Gesell.

Und plappert Antwort,
   Und ist so dumm,
Und geht und glaubt ihr —
   Weiß nicht warum.

43

THE MILLER'S SONG.

JUST as the water
   The mill-wheel twirls,
My little sweetheart
   My senses whirls.

She chats, caresses,
   And chides me ill,
And laughs and changes
   My mood at will.

And if I murmur,
   She talks so fast ;
And her companion
   Gets cross at last.

He rattles an answer,
   Some silly cry,
And goes and believes her —
   He knows not why.

Doch sie hüpft weiter.

Des Lebens froh,

Und macht's dem Nächsten

Dann wieder so.

Der Bach ist treulos,

Das Mägdlein schlecht —

O Mühlenräder!

O Müller's Knecht!

But on she capers,
  Through life so gay,
And treats the next one
  The selfsame way.

The brook is faithless,
  The maiden coy —
O whirling mill-wheel!
  O miller boy!

Beim Füttern.

Wie duftig riecht's im Stall! Die Kühe strecken
  Die Hälse lang, mit ungeduld'gem Brummen,
  Den Klee begrüßend mit zufriednem Summen,
Und wie die Nasen sie so glänzend lecken!

Die schönen Thiere mit dem Sammetkleide,
  Im goldnen Licht der Sommermorgensonne,
  Mit quellend unerschöpftem Lebensbronne,
Mit goldnen Sammetaugen voller Leide.

Und stumm erdulden dann sie beim Gebären
  Der Schmerzen Pein. Wie sind die and'ren Kühe
  Voll Mitgefühl! Daß spärlich und mit Mühe
Sie an dem Tage brummend Milch gewähren.

Das herz'ge Kälbchen muß ich nun belügen;
  Die Hand im Eimer. Meine Finger taugen
  Als Entertrug. Des zarten Mäulchens Saugen
Fühl' ich so warm mit innigem Vergnügen.

52

FODDER-TIME.

How sweet the manger smells! The cows all listen
    With outstretched necks, and with impatient
      lowing;
    They greet the clover, their content now showing—
And how they lick their noses till they glisten!

The velvet-coated beauties do not languish
    Beneath the morning's golden light that's breaking,
    The unexhausted spring of life awaking,
Their golden eyes of velvet full of anguish.

They patiently endure their pains. Bestowing
    Their sympathy, the other cows are ruing
    Their unproductive udders and renewing
At milking-time their labor and their lowing.

And now I must deceive the darling bossy —
    With hand in milk must make it suck my finger.
    Its tender lips cling close like joys that linger,
And feel so warm with dripping white and flossy.

Dieselbe Hand, die mir die Leute küssen

    Voll Ehrfurcht, und die malt und spielt und

        dichtet —

    O hätt' ich immer nur den Klee geschichtet;

Das unschuldsvolle Kuhkind nähren müssen!

This very hand my people with devotion

    Do kiss, which paints and plays and writes more-

        over —

    I would it had done naught but pile the clover

To feed the kine tnat know no base emotion !

Beim Molken.

So! So! Liebe Braune! nun gieb schön her!
 Dann kriegt dein Kälbchen auch um so mehr!

Und daß Du's weißt: von den Kälbchen all'
Ist Dein's das schönste vom ganzen Stall!

Schwarzbraun ist es, mit weißem Stern!
Gelt? Du willst's haben, Du leckst so gern?

Da! küß Dein Kleines! und brumme nicht Du!
Ich laß' es doch nicht zum Trinken zu!

Uns' Frau nennt's Pollux; das wär' Latein,
Ich denk': auf Deutsch wird's wohl Bullochs sein.

MILKING-TIME.

So! so! pretty Brownie, come let it down!
  I'll give the more milk to your bossy brown!

You know well enough in yonder stall
Your bossy's the prettiest boss of them all,

With its dark-brown coat and the star on its brow.
What's this? You insist you must lick it now?

There! Kiss your little one; now be still!
Not yet can the bossy drink its fill!

Madame calls it Pollux; you know the name;
'Tis the Latin for Bullock — it's all the same!

57

Am Pfluge.

Hier ist der Ackergrund so tief und schwer;
    Acht Ochsen ziehen einen Pflug mit Mühe,
    Und weiß gekleidet geh'n in kühler Frühe,
In heißer Gluth, der Mann, die Frau, daher.

Kein Dung. Sie führt, er drückt die Pflugschaar sehr —
    Auf daß aus Erdenschooß ihr Kind erblühe,
    Gebiert im Feld sie, eh' der Tag verglühe,
Kommt barfuß mit dem Säugling dann daher.

Einst war die Nacht gereist ich, im Gewälde
    Von Baierland erwacht, der Heimath zu
Flog ich zum Rhein, zum Mütterlein in Bälde!
    „Daß ich in Deutschland bin, Gott! zeig' mir's Du!“
Zwölf Häuflein Dung, auf tellergroßem Felde,
    Im Kittel, pflügt' ein Mann mit seiner Kuh!

58

THE PLOWING.

THE soil is here so deep and hard, their might
   Eight oxen spend and strain beneath the plowing;
   And here at morn and when the sun is glowing,
The farmer and his wife toil, clad in white.

No dung.   She guides, he holds the plow down tight —
   And there her baby, like some blossom growing
   From Mother Earth, is born.   Barefoot and bowing
Beneath its weight, she bears it home at night.

One night, in the Bavarian forest waking,
   I journeyed homeward hasting to the Rhine,
Myself to my sweet mother swift betaking.
   "That this my country is, God give the sign!"
Twelve heaps of dung, in frock a farmer breaking
   His tiny field with plow and cow in line.

Im Klee.

Mit rothen Tüchlein im rothen Mohn,
    Zur Mittagsruh,
Da nicken sich kichernd im Flüsterton
    Drei Mägdlein zu.

Der Bursch dort drüben im andern Feld
    Hat hergeseh'n,
Und dreht noch immer die Augen — gelt? —
    Im Weitergeh'n.

Und singt und schlendert von Ungefähr
    Noch 'mal vorbei,
Und schaut verstohlen so wieder her:
    „Noch immer Drei!"

Dann singt er lauter und eilt davon:
    „Ich geh' schon, geh'!
Der Kukuk hole den ganzen Mohn
    Im schönen Klee!"

IN CLOVER.

WITH kerchiefs red where the poppies grow,
    In midday shades,
Nod each to other and titter low
    Three little maids.

The lad who yonder strays to and fro
    Here casts his eye,
And ever he looks askance — oho ? —
    In passing by.

And sings and saunters past as by chance
    Continually,
And sees with every stolen glance :
    "Still ever three !"

Then louder he sings and away he goes,
    " I'll be a rover !
The devil take each poppy that grows
    In pretty clover !"

Juli.

Die Blumenhäuptchen begrüßen sich
   In meinem Garten und nicken;
Und duften erröthend und müssen sich
   Viel Liebesboten schicken.

Die armen Blumen! sie möchten gern
   Einander zärtlich umschlingen,
Drum senden sie also den Duft von Fern,
   Sich zu auf der Lüfte Schwingen.

In meinem Garten da schwebt und bebt
   Ein Wunderwerden lebendig;
In meinem Garten da spinnt und webt
   Der Liebe Leben beständig.

JULY.

MY garden-flowers, in summer bloom,
   With common greetings are bending;
And each to other, 'mid blushing perfume,
   Their bearers of love are sending.

The poor, poor flowers! they long to share
   With each their tender embraces;
So send from afar, on the wings of the air,
   Their scents through the garden spaces.

There hovers and hangs, among the leaves,
   A marvel that ceaseth never;
Among the leaves love spins and weaves
   The strands of life forever.

63

Der Sämann.

Auffaugt die Sonne milde den Dunst der feuchten Erde,
  Die tief und duftig wartet auf's neue Saatempfangen;
    Kornschnitt und Stoppelfeuer und Ernte sind vergangen;
Vorbei dem Untergrunde des scharfen Pflugs Beschwerde.

Der Sämann schreitet einsam und ernst auf brauner Erde —
  Zwei Schritte, dann die Handvoll. Kein Zaudern und kein Bangen;
    Die kleinen Vögel folgen und picken voll Verlangen.
Er streut; doch Gottes Sonne muß gnädig rufen: „Werde!"

Und ob der Frost sie tödtet, ob Dürre sie vernichtet,
  Im Frühlingswinde wiegend die Halme auferstehen,
Und in dem nächsten Herbste der Körner Gold erschichtet.

64

THE SOWER.

BENEATH the mild sun vanish the vapor's last wet
traces,

   And for the autumn sowing the mellow soil lies
steeping;

   The stubble fires have faded and ended is the reaping;

The piercing plow has leveled the rough resisting places.

The solitary sower along the brown field paces —

   Two steps and then a handful, a rhythmic motion
keeping;

   The eager sparrows follow, now pecking and now
peeping.

He sows; but all the increase accomplished by God's
grace is.

And whether frost be fatal or drought be devastating,

   The blades rise green and slender for spring-time
winds to flutter,

As time of golden harvest the coming fall awaiting.

Es sieht die Fragen Keiner, die auf den Lippen flehen,
Die bangenden Gedanken, die schwere Sorge dichtet.
  Mit fester Hand muß schweigend durch's Feld der Sä=
mann gehen.

None see the silent yearnings the sower's lips half
 utter,

The carping care he suffers, distressing thoughts cre-
 ating.

With steady hand he paces afield without a mutter.

Schifferlied.

Bergunter geht's im Mondlicht,
   Bergauf im Sonnenbrand;
Bergunter auf den Wellen,
   Bergauf im tiefen Sand.

Bergunter frei am Steuer,
   Das Pfeifchen glimmt im Mund;
Bergauf da zieht, als Saumthier,
   Man Brust und Lenden wund.

Was hilft mir's, wenn ich heute
   Des Stromes König bin,
Schleich' morgen ich als Bettler
   Verachtet an ihm hin?

Um meine Lustfahrt schließt sich
   Furchlos die Wasserflur;
Vom keuchend tiefen Schreiten
   Bleibt lang im Sand die Spur.

THE BOATMAN'S SONG.

DOWN stream 'tis all by moonlight,
Up stream at blazing noon,
Down stream upon the ripples,
Up stream through sandy dune.

Down stream, the helm held loosely,
A pipe between the lips;
Up stream, like beast one straineth
And galls the breast and hips.

What boots it that I seem like
The river's king to-day,
If to-morrow like a beggar,
Despised, I tug away?

My pleasuring leaves no furrow
Upon the water-plain;
The marks of struggling footsteps
Long in the sand remain.

Fischer.

In Holland war's, grau tost die See,
  Grau war der Himmel drob verhangen,
  Grauweiß der Strand wie Herbstesweh,
Der Wind, die Wellen hangen.

Dort kommt es blutroth, fern heran,
  Ein Segel! Auf! die Fischer! Frauen
Wie Möwen stürmen her; wer kann
  Wohl seine Pink erschauen!

Auftauchen wie die Flotte dicht
  Nun Boot an Boot vor Wolkenballen,
Mit Hoffnungsangst im Angesicht
  Heran die Frauen wallen.

In weißen Hauben stehn sie da,
  Zu Hunderten gereiht am Strande,
Mit Kindern, — Wer den Gatten sah?
  Wer ausblieb? Welcher lande?

70

THE FISHERMAN.

IN Holland 'twas.   The sea was gray,
  And gray the heavy hanging heaven;
Gray-white the shore with autumn spray,
  The wind and waves gray even.

Afar a blood-red cloud streams out —
  A sail! The fishing trip is over!
Like gulls the women flock about:
  Who can her boat discover!

Sail after sail from out the gloom
  Before the flaming cloud now passes;
Near rush the wan-faced women whom
  An anxious hope harasses.

With children, and with hooded head
  In hundreds on the shore they're standing;
Who saw her spouse?   Which one is dead?
  Which one will now be landing?

Ein Reiter jagt im Schaum daher,
　　Sein Schimmel gleicht dem Gischt der Welle,
Ist sattellos, das Haupt ist leer,
　　Und barfuß der Geselle.

Es trieft von Wasser sein Gewand,
　　Er fängt im Wurf die schweren Seile,
Und trägt sie von des Schiffes Rand,
　　Zum Ufersand, in Eile.

Er jagt — ihm fliegt sein blondes Haar —
　　Im Sturm zu all den braunen Pinken,
Und zeigt den Harrenden — 's ist klar! —
　　Mit einem raschen Winken.

Sie schrei'n die Zahl vom Schiff hinab,
　　Er hebt die Finger, und die Wogen
Vom Gaule spülen ihn herab,
　　Er schwingt sich auf im Bogen.

A rider through the foam hastes there;
  His steed is flecked with white and yellow,
His saddle's gone, his head is bare,
  And bare-foot is the fellow.

With water all his clothing drips;
  He casts the rope where he would fain land
In haste to drag them from the ship's
  Deck forth upon the mainland.

With streaming hair he presses near
  Where all the other boats are beating;
And to those waiting signs — 'tis clear! —
  His one quick nod repeating.

They shriek the number of his ship;
  He becks and 'neath the billows, flinging
Him from his racer, seems to dip,
  Then on the crest goes swinging.

„Schon zwanzig Wochen," sprach ein Weib,
    „Ist fern mein Gatte dort im Meere."
Die Mutter nickt — „Am Leben bleib'
    Ich, bis er wiederkehre."

Ein Schiffsherr auf den Nacken läßt
    Dem jungen Mann sich bis zum Strande;
Sein Weib umschlingt ihn jauchzend fest:
    Sein Kind tanzt auf dem Sande, —

Und haut, vor Freude ungerügt,
    Den Vater in die derben Beine,
Der fühlt es nicht, erzählt vergnügt,
    Dem Rheder von der Leine.

Die Ebbe fällt, das letzte Boot
    Kann trotz der Eile nicht mehr landen.
„Ja," spricht das Weib, „En für* Stück Brod.
    Und scheitern oder stranden!"

---

* En für = ein sauer.

"These twenty weeks," so spake a wife,
  "Far off my spouse has sailed the ocean."
His mother nods: "I'll cling to life
  Till he's here, with devotion."

The owner of the ship at last
  Bears the young man safe to the strand there;
His wife shrieks out and holds him fast;
  His child skips o'er the sand there.

He lets it pelt his legs with shells,
  Unchided though behaving badly,
Nor does he feel it as he tells
  About the rope so gladly.

The tide recedes, the last crew fail,
  In spite of haste, at landing.
"Yes," speaks the wife; "His bread is stale,
  His fate — shipwrecked or stranding!"

Den Säugling an der Bruſt, ſo ſteht
　Und harrt dort Eine, ſcharf vom Winde
Umflattert. Wie ſie ſorgſam dreht,
　Zum Schutz dem kleinen Kinde!

Mitleidig ſprach ich: „Habt Ihr noch
　Der Kindlein mehr, wie dieſes ſchöne?"
„Mehr?" rief ſie ſtolz und ſtreckt' ſich hoch:
　„Mit dem hab' ich eilf Söhne!"

„Eilf Söhne!" Wie ein Schrei entfloh'n
　War neidvoll mir das Wort vom Munde;
Sie wandten ſich nach jenem Ton
　Und drängten in die Runde.

Ein Glitzern in der Augen Grau,
　Frug mich das Weib, das Kind am Herzen:
„Wie viele habt denn Ihr, me* Frau?"
　Hochmüthig klang's, wie Scherzen.

---

* me = meine.

With babe at breast where winds sweep wild,
　There stands and waits and stares another.
How turns to shield her little child
　That anxious loving mother!

" Pray hast thou " — spake in pity I —
　" More children sweet as this one even? "
" More? " called she proud, her head raised high;
　" Of sons I have eleven."

" Eleven Sons! " I shrieked the word
　In envy; how it did astound me!
They turned then who my cry had heard
　And gathered close around me.

She asked — her eyes were gleaming gray,
　Upon her heart her babe was resting:
" How many, lady, hast thou pray? " —
　It sounded like gay jesting.

Wie viel? Sie fah'n mich an, Verkauf
  Und Meer vergeſſend, Ebb' und Schimmel —
Ich ſchwieg, hob einen Finger auf
  Und deutete 'gen Himmel.

How many? Staring they forget the sea
 And trade and tide and foam-horse even; —
I raised one finger silently
 And pointed up toward heaven.

Beim Spinnen.

Ein Mägdlein schwebt dahin durch's Feld,
  Den grünen Krug anf's Haupt gestellt,
Die rothe Nelk' im rothen Mund,
Der Leib so schlank, die Brust so rund;
Geschürzt eilt sie von hinnen,
  Beim Spinnen.

Die Kunkel ihr im Gürtel steckt,
Wie niedlich sie das Händchen reckt,
Die Spindel tanzt und kommt und flieht;
Sie horcht auf's Vogelmaienlied,
Auf aller Bächlein Rinnen,
  Beim Spinnen.

Am Nußbaum bei dem Brunnen steht
Der schlanke Bursch, und harrt und späht,

SPINNING SONG.

THROUGH yonder field there fares a maid,
 A water-jar upon her head,
A pink between her rosy lips;
Her form is lithe, and light she trips;
She hastes away so winning,
  While spinning.

Her distaff from her belt depends —
How simply she her hand extends!
The dancing spindle flies along;
She listens to the May-bird's song,
Or brooklets gaily dinning,
  While spinning.

Beneath the tree the brook runs by
A tall lad stands and waits to spy:

Der Gurt so breit, das Hemde weiß,
Das Haar ist schwarz, das Auge heiß, —
Was wird sie nun beginnen
    Beim Spinnen?

„Jetzt lauf mir nicht vorbei so toll!
Hast keine Hand, der Krug ist voll;
Die Nelke stehl' ich mir zuerst,
Und ob Du Dich auch biegst und wehrst,
Den Kuß will ich gewinnen
    Beim Spinnen!"

Sie kommt von unter'm Baum heraus,
Und sieht mir so verändert aus —
Fort ist der Kinderübermuth,
Das Auge blickt voll tiefer Gluth,
In traumverlornem Sinnen,
    Beim Spinnen!

His chest is broad, his blouse is white,
His hair is black, his eyes are bright, —
But what is she beginning
    While spinning?

"Now pass not by so quick and coy;
The jar and flax your hands employ;
So first I'll steal the pink away.
Though in defence you stand at bay,
A kiss you'll find me winning
    While spinning."

She comes forth from beneath the tree,
And she appears so changed to me —
Her childish confidence is dead,
Her eye is full of passion, fed
By thoughts and dreams beginning
    While spinning.

Uhrmacherlied.

Mir ist es wie unserm Herrgott fast
   In all dem Rädergetriebe,
Ich hab' an dem Zeug so meine Lust
   Und meine Liebe!

Geheimnißvoll ist zusammengericht,'
   Mit Schrauben und Feilen und Schleifen.
Ein Stoß! Dann geht es auf einmal nicht,
   Und will nicht greifen!

Und mühvoll sinnt man bei Tag und Nacht,
   Wäre gern vor Aerger gestorben,
Da hat ein Tölpel 'was d'ran gemacht,
   Und Alles verdorben!

Der Uhrmacher droben hat's gut gefügt,
   Und sauber geschraubt und verzieret;
Die Menschen haben nur, stillvergnügt,
   Es stracks ruiniret.

THE CLOCKMAKER'S SONG.

I SEEM like the Lord himself in the cogs,
  In the wheel, the spring and the lever;
My heart beats with it as on it jogs,
  And will forever.

'Tis made by a wondrous process in shops,
  With screws and filing and rasping.
A shock! — Then on the second it stops,
  The cogs not clasping.

The careworn maker thinks night and day
  He's ready to die of vexation,
Because some young blockhead accomplished in play
  Its ruination.

The Clock-man above is a master-hand;
  His work's well fitted and polished;
But mortals delight to see what's planned
  At once demolished!

Dann kommt der Meister und macht's zurecht;
  Euch schmerzt das Feilen und Passen;
Ihr schreit und jammert, das Werk sei schlecht,
  Der Schlag zum Hassen!

Doch wenn das Uhrwerk zu Ende geht,
  Dann wollt Ihr vor Bangen verzagen;
Dann schiebt Ihr den Zeiger: „Noch mehr!" — zu spät:
  Es hat euch am Kragen!

Then the maker comes and repairs it again;
　You're pained by the filing and fitting;
The work is miserably done, you complain;
　You hate the hitting.

When the clock's worn out, as decreed by fate,
　You'll hear the dreaded "'Tis time!"
You'll push the hands: "Go on!" Too late!
　It's got you this time!

Der Farbenreiber.

Der kleine Farbenreiber vermißt sich, ohne Zieren,
   An seiner Meister Bildern die Fehler scharf zu
   rügen.
„Hier alte Farben, Junge! Du sollst uns zum Ver-
   gnügen
Nun selber etwas malen, statt uns zu critisiren.“

Und heftig thut die Leinwand der Knabe grau ver-
   schmieren:
„Ein Thurm im Nebel ist das, in unbestimmten
   Zügen!“
Hohn lacht er: „Ohne Eisen kann schwerlich einer
   pflügen,
„Ich will mit schlechtem Werkzeug nicht meine Zeit
   verlieren!“

THE little color-grinder full wantonly was sneering
At all his master's pictures, their errors sharp
upbraiding.
"Take these old colors, youngster; your smartness
cease parading:
Do you yourself paint something, and be not over-
bearing."

The ardent boy his canvass with gray begins a-
smearing:
"A tower that is, but misty, with outlines dim and
fading."
He scoffs: "One must have iron for ploughing and
for spading;
I will not waste my vigor with good-for-nothing gearing."

„Hier haſt Du gute Pinſel und Farben; doch nun zeige

    Zum letzten Mal Dein Können." — Da wird der

       Künſtler wach:

Er malt drei kleine Spatzen, im Schnee auf dürrem

    Zweige.

Die Maler kommen ſtaunend: „Das macht ihm Keiner

    nach!"

    Für Gold ward's gleich erhandelt, ſein Kümmern ging

    zur Neige:

Es ward der kleine Lehrling der große Achenbach.

"Take these new paints and brushes, and once for all
>   redouble
Your efforts."   Lo, the artist now first is animate:
He paints three little sparrows, in snow, above the
>   stubble.

The painters are dumbfounded: "Him none can
>   imitate?"
It brought him gold directly, and banished all his
>   trouble:
That small apprentice lad became Achenbach the
>   great.

Bäckerlied.

Wer wollte noch leben,
  Wenn's Brod nicht wär',
Den Krug noch heben?
  Ihn freut's nicht mehr!

Das Fleisch wär' fade,
  Kein Wein wär' süß,
Mir wär's nicht schade
  Ums Paradies!

Dort giebt's kein Feuer
  Kein Ofen nicht,
Da fahr' ich treuer
  Zur Hölle schlicht,

Und hole täglich
  Mein Brod heraus.
Es sieht doch kläglich
  Im Himmel aus!

THE BAKER'S SONG.

WHO'D live on with pleasure
    That had no bread?
Or drain his measure?
    His joy'd be dead!

There'd be no savor
    In meat or wine;
I'd scorn the flavor
    Of things divine.

No fire's up yonder,
    No oven for dough,
So quick I'd wander
    To hell below.

And daily I'd fetch it —
    My batch of bread —
My outlook how wretched
    In Heaven instead!

Und hätt' eine Krone
Und Scepter ich,
Und gäb's auf dem Throne
Kein Brod für mich —

Ich ging als Wand'rer
Davon, allein;
Es soll ein Andrer
Hier König sein!

Wie duftet's eben —
Ihr Wangen roth!
Das Brod soll leben,
Das liebe Brod!

Were crown to me given,
  And scepter beside,
Were a throne mine, even,
  And bread denied,

I'd flee, ever straying
  Afar, alone,
Another here swaying
  Upon my throne.

The sweet smell of thee!
  Thy cheeks how red!
O Bread, I love thee!
  So, long live Bread!

Seilerlied.

Wie's Spinnlein nehm' ich vom Leibe
   Den Hanf heraus,
Doch mein Geschäft ich betreibe
   Mit Radgebraus.

Wie Spinnweb' sollen die Seile
   'Gen Himmel steh'n,
Doch sollen in Sturmeseile
   D'rauf Menschen geh'n.

D'ran sollen sie schweben und hangen,
   Vom Meer bedroht;
D'ran sollen sie beten und bangen,
   In Todesnoth.

Dort werden sie lachen und pfeifen
   Dem Ocean,
Da Hungerschrecken mich greifen —
   Mich armen Mann!

THE ROPE-MAKER'S SONG.

I, LIKE the spiders a spinning,
  My hemp play out;
But I work with the dinning
  Of wheels about.

My cords, like webs toward Heaven,
  Shall stand sublime;
Yet there in tempests even
  Shall sailors climb.

And there they'll hover and quiver,
  Nor mind the roar;
And there they'll pray and shiver
  By death's cold shore.

They'll laugh and scoff at the booming
  Made by the sea,
The dread of hunger consuming
  Poor wretched me!

Töpferlied.

Schwirr Du im Kreise!
  Ewig die Reise,
    Dreh doch!
Nimmer zu rasten,
Ewig zu hasten —
    Geh doch!
Unten hin tret' ich,
Oben hin knet' ich
    Dreh Doch!
Nie darfst Du matt sein,
Nie darfst Du satt sein —
    Geh doch!
Was wir auch kochen,
Bald wird's zerbrochen —
    Dreh doch!
Trinken wird's nimmer,
Dursten nur schlimmer —
    Geh doch!

THE POTTER'S SONG.

ROUND thou art wending!
  Never an ending!
    Twirl on!
No time wasting,
Ever hasting,
    Whirl on!
Under treading,
Over kneading —
    Twirl on!
Never dare weary,
Always be cheery,
    Whirl on!
Though we may make it,
Some one will break it —
    Twirl on!
Though it drinks never,
Thirsteth it ever —
    Whirl on!

Dich soll sie schnelle.

Tragen zur Quelle —

Dreh doch!

Dir von Mund nippen

Willige Lippen —

Geh doch!

Das man die Krüge

Alle zerschlüge!

Dreh doch!

Wollt ihr den Haufen

Einzeln verkaufen!

Geh doch!

Dies für ein Küßchen,

Drei für die Füßchen —

Dreh doch!

Und für die Dicken

Müßt sie ersticken!

Geh doch!

Thee shall she carry
Springward, and tarry —
Twirl on!
Lipping with kisses
Ware such as this is —
Whirl on!
Till we just take it,
Jealous, and break it.
Twirl on!
Gladly we'd sell her
All and then tell her —
Whirl on!
This for a kiss, now,
Those three for this, now,
Twirl on!
And for this other
Must she just smother —
Whirl on!

Mosaik.

Venedig träumt.   Die Markuskirche breitet
   Die gold'ne Dämm'rung über Wunderschätze;
   Als ob er sich an soviel Schönheit letze,
Stiehlt sich ein Sonnenstrahl herab und gleitet

Dort Christi Haupt entlang, und bebt und schreitet
   Hin, ob dem Boden, in die alten Plätze,
   Das Chorstuhlholz vergoldend, d'rein sich setze
Der Zeiten Majestät, von Gott geleitet.

Und all' die Pracht kommt aus der schmalen Kammer,
   Darein ein Mensch der farb'gen Splitter Gleißen
Mühsam zusammenlegt mit winz'ger Klammer,

   Der grüne Schirm deckt unterm Haar, dem weißen,
Der Augen schwindend Licht. Was thut der Jammer?
   Das Werk ist ewig — Gott hat's gut geheißen!

MOSAIC.

THE island city sleeps. The twilight rideth
   Gold-shod above San Marco's treasure-plunder;
  As if it would enjoy this golden wonder,
A sunbeam stealeth in and softly glideth

Along Christ's head and trembleth there and strideth
   To earth where columns cut the light asunder;
  It gildeth, sent of God, the choir, where, under
The dome, the glory of the ages bideth.

High in an attic room this decoration
   In splendor wakens, where a man, deft-handed,
Sets tiny bits of bright illumination —

   To shield his fading sight, his white locks banded
With a green shade. — What profits lamentation?
  The work's eternal — God hath so commanded!

Tapezierer.

(Brummchor.)

Den Mund voll Nägel
    Wie singt man da?
In Stoff vergraben
    Wie klingt es da?

Bald nah der Decke,
    Gebückt auf Knien,
Bis reicht der Teppich,
    Verrückt zu ziehn.

Den schönen Damen,
    So reif und zart,
Ist gutes Polster
    Nur steif und hart.

Und tief verhängen
    Der Scheibe Licht,
Man zeigt sein Antlitz
    Bei Leibe nicht!

THE UPHOLSTERER.

(A Muttering Chorus.)

WHO could, his mouth full
  Of tac s, still sing?
Thus deep in drapery
  A bell couldn't ring!

It almost reaches;
  Come, kneel, my lad
And stretch the carpet;
  Now tug like mad!

Fastidious ladies
  Declare the stuff
On this fine cushion
  Too stiff and rough.

These window-hangings
  Come down so far
They let no passer
  See who you are.

Wär't Ihr noch toller
  Von Eitelkeit,
Das macht dem Handwerk
  Den Beutel weit.

Wollt Ihr verhüllen
  Den Schein der Jahr,
Das giebt mir Kleider
  Der kleinen Schaar.

Und weil Ihr ruhet
  So weich und warm,
Sind Bänk' in Schulen
  Für Reich und Arm!

Were you still wilder
  With vanity,
'Twould fill the pockets
  Of such as we.

If asked to refurbish
  The wear of years,
It gives me clothes for
  My little dears.

Because you're resting
  At ease, secure,
We have school-benches
  For rich and poor.

Vergolder.

Da seht mir nur die Leute an —
    Wie undankbar!
Der Rembrandt war ein braver Mann,
    Das ist wohl wahr!

Der Rubens war ja auch nicht faul —
    Die Zeit bedacht!
Und Wouwermann hat manchen Gaul
    Recht brav gemacht!

Ganz sauber hat Murillo ja
    Und Reusch gemalt;
Doch wenn man Makart's Preise sah —
    Recht schlecht bezahlt! —

Doch sagt: Wo blieb euch der Effekt?
    Ich mein den Scharm!
Der ist im Rahmen d'rin versteckt,
    Im Goldton warm.

THE GILDER.

JUST look now at the public once —
    A thankless crew!
That Rembrandt was no simple dunce,
    Indeed is true.

And Rubens painted far from ill —
    For that dull age!
And Wouwermann's fine horses still
    Are quite the rage.

Murillo painted soberly
    And Reusch as well;
But if you Makart's prices see —
    How poor they sell! —

You say: Wherein lies your effect?
    The charm alone
Is in the frame with which it's decked —
    Its warm gold tone.

Die ganzen Maler sind erst 'was,
 Bin ich dabei!
Dem Raphael ginget, ohne Spaß,
 Ihr kalt vorbei,

Hielt er nicht schön im Rahmen sich!
 An Gold gebricht's:
Die größten Künstler ohne mich
 Sind alle Nichts!

If aught of any painter 's heard,
    Lo, there am I!
You'd pass — this is no idle word —
    The Raphaels by,

Unless they were set off by me
    In frames like these;
The greatest artists else would be
    Nonentities!

Zimmermaler.

Als wenn sie mir angewachsen wär',
   So wandl' ich mit meiner Leiter einher,
      Und singe!

Und mal' Euch reiche Farben hinein,
   Mit satten Schatten und Goldton fein,
      Und singe!

Das fliegt mir Alles so aus der Hand,
An Holzgetäfel, Alhambrawand,
      Beim Singen!

Das wird ganz künstlerisch fein gestimmt,
Hier etwas kälter, daß dort es glimmt,
      Beim Singen!

Die Praktischen haben geschimpft, gelacht,
Geseufzt, daß Luxus ins Leben gebracht —
      Drum sing ich!

THE PAINTER.

A S though to my back it had chanced to grow,
I carry my ladder wherever I go,
      And sing!

I paint for you colors as rich as made,
With a fine gold tone and just the right shade,
      And sing!

With a twist of the wrist I accomplish it all —
A wainscoting or an Alhambra wall —
      While singing!

'Twill be well toned and artistic, you know,
Here a little bit cold, so that there it may glow
      While I sing!

The Old School has scoffed and sighed at the thought
That luxury into life has been brought —
      I sing!

Vier kahle Wände und d'rin ein Loch
Ist auch ein Zimmer und einfach doch —
Zum Brummen!

Four naked walls with a hole for a door

Make a room, 'tis true; and simple, what's more —

    For growling!

Der Landbriefträger.

Es thaut. Der Schnee ballt braun sich auf Graben,
        Feld und Wegen,
    Es trieft die Vogelbeere, der Schlamm ist tief und
        weich,
    Die Wolken hängen bleiern, der Abendschein ist bleich,
Es glänzt wie Bachesbette das Licht auf allen Stegen.

Und einsam auf der Straße stapft dort ein mühsam
        Regen,
    Es hinkt der Bote frierend, die Tasche scheint nicht
        reich —
    Ein armer Brief an Arme, verkrumpelt, alt — ganz
        gleich,
Er muß an's Ziel. Der Bote hinkt müd' dem Dorf
        entgegen.

Er pocht. Da öffnet schüchtern ein Mütterchen: „Im
        Leben

THE COUNTRY LETTER-CARRIER.

IT thaws. On field and roadway the packing drifts
    have faded;
  The service-berry drips and the slush is deep and
    stale;
  The clouds hang low and leaden; the evening glow
    is pale;
The paths gleam like a brooklet whose bed is all
    unshaded.

Along the highway trudges a messenger; unaided
  He limps and halts and shivers; his bag holds
    little mail —
  A single wretched letter all crumpled, old, and frail —
He must push on; the village he nears now, lame
    and jaded.

He knocks. A timid woman admits him: "Till now.
    never

Schreibt Keiner mir? O Himmel! Mein Sohn!
  Gieb eilends her!
Er kommt! Uns ist geholfen!" Die alten Hände
  beben —

„Du Gottesbote! näher, setz' Dich zur Flamme her,
Ich will von meinem Reichthum Dir Deinen Antheil
  geben."
Der arme Landbriefträger hat warm und hinkt nicht
  mehr.

Had I a letter! Heavens! My boy! Quick, give
    it here!
He's coming! Now we're happy!" Her aged muscles
    quiver —

"God sent you here. Be seated and warm your-
    self: Come near;
A share of my possessions are yours to keep forever."
    The postman limps no longer, warmed by the
    woman's cheer.

Der Sandträger.

Sand! Sand! Sand! Sand!
   Ich bin so müd', Ihr Leut!
Hat Keiner Sand gestreut
Den ganzen, langen, kalten Tag,
Da frostzitternd ich stand
Und Lasten trag'!

Sand! Sand! Sand! Sand!
Es sind noch fünf zu Haus;
Die Mutter die schafft d'raus;
Dann weinen sie, die kleinen Kind',
Weil sie mich ausgesandt,
Und hungrig sind.

Sand! Sand! Sand! Sand!
Dort liegt das Brod zu Hauf!
Daß ich nur eines kauf',

THE SAND-CARRIER.

SAND! Sand! Sand! Sand!
  Good Sirs, I'm almost dead,
For no one sand has spread
The live-long day, so cold and drear
That 'neath my load I stand
      And shiver here.

Sand! Sand! Sand! Sand!
Five more at home there are.
While Mother toils afar,
The little ones, who let me go
With naught to eat at hand,
      Are weeping so!

Sand! Sand! Sand! Sand!
There bread in heaps doth lie;
That I one loaf may buy

So nimmt Ihr Leut' den Sand mir ab,
Weil ich so weit gerannt
Und Hunger hab!

Sand! Sand! Sand! Sand!
Der Abend bricht herein;
Nun friert es Stein und Bein;
Doch heim ich nimmer gehen kann,
Sie harren unverwandt
Und schau'n mich an!

Sand! Sand! Sand! Sand!
Das Kleine jauchzt und lacht:
„Was hast Du mitgebracht?“
Die Mutter weint und sagt kein Wort,
Am kalten Heerdesrand —
Dann schleich' ich fort.

Sand! Sand! Sand! Sand!
Die Thräne friert zu Eis,
Ich ruf' es noch ganz leis',

Do take my sand, so kind you are,

For I'm so hungry and

I've trudged so far.

Sand! Sand! Sand! Sand!

The daylight now has flown,

Now freezes stone and bone;

But home poor I can never flee;

For those there still do stand

And gaze at me.

Sand! Sand! Sand! Sand!

My child shouts out with joy:

"What have you brought your boy?"

His mother weeps — she cannot say —

At the cold hearth-stone and —

I steal away!

Sand! Sand! Sand! Sand!

My tears freeze like the snow:

My call is now quite low.

Die Häuser locken hell und warm,

Doch öffnet keine Hand —

Dort winkt ein Arm!

Sand! Sand! Sand! Sand!

The houses gleam with welcome warm,
But opens no kind hand —
   There waves an arm!
Sand! Sand! Sand! Sand!

Die Scheuerfrau.

Wenn's nur nicht Christabend wär',
 Und gar so viel Lichter,
Und all' die Tische so schwer,
 So froh die Gesichter.

Wär's nicht so trostlos zuhaus,
 Und würden nicht weinen
Und verlangten nicht so hinaus
 Die hungernden Kleinen,

Und ihre Wänglein so schmal,
 Die heut' Nichts zum Essen
Wenn die nur ahnten die Qual
 Die heut' mich vergessen!

Doch ich komme zu leise herein,
 Zum schmutz'gen Geschäfte
Und verbrauche bei Dämmerschein
 Die schwindenden Kräfte.

126

THE CHARWOMAN.

IF only 'twere not Christmas Eve,
  Nor bright other places,
Nor loaded the boards I perceive,
  Nor happy the faces,

And not so wretched at home,
  And none of this whining
And begging for bread when I come
  By little cheeks pining

To-day for hunger again,
  To deeply depress me!
If they, who forget now my pain,
  Could see it distress me!

Too listlessly come I and go;
  All dirty I never
Must faint in the twilight glow
  But toil on forever.

Mir find die Sechfe zu fchwer,
  Die bleichen Gefichter!
Wenn's nur nicht Chriftabend wär',
  Und alle die Lichter!

Six children I have to relieve —
    How blanched are their faces!
If only 'twere not Christmas Eve,
    Nor bright other places!

Der Bläser.

Mit meinem Hauch in rothe Gluth,
   Mit Aug' und Hand in Flammenwuth,
      Blas! Blas!

Und was Ihr füllt und singend leert
Hat mir das Lebensmark verzehrt:
      Glas! Glas!

Ich setz' es vor Euch an den Mund
Und schwing' es hoch im Kreise rund —
      Blas! Blas!

Und was mein letzter Hauch gemacht,
Ihr schlagt's entzwei und singt und lacht —
      Glas! Glas!

Und bei der weißen Flammen Schein
Denk' ich der kleinen Kinder mein —
      Blas! Blas!

THE GLASS-BLOWER.

I BREATHE into the red-hot heat;
My eye and hand its fury meet —
    Blow! Blow!

The glass you fill and singing drain
Has sapped my life and might amain —
    Glass! Glass!

I'm first to put my lips to it there
And swing it circling high in air —
    Blow! Blow!

My last breath makes the very thing
You break in two, then laugh and sing —
    Glass! Glass!

Now softly by the white-hot flame
I call my children each by name —
    Blow! Blow!

Die Gluth wird kalt, bald lieg' ich dort,

Man fegt mich mit den Scherben fort —

Glas! Glas!

The fire grows cold; I'll die, no doubt;

With broken glass they'll sweep me out —

Glass! Glass!

Am Webstuhl.

Im blütheweißen Hemd und rothem Rocke,
  Im Schleier, der zur Erde niederfließt,
  Das Schiffchen jagend, das wie's Mäuslein schießt,
Die kleine Hand so fest am langen Stocke,

Webt Spinngeweb aus eigner Seidenflocke
  Die schöne Bäuerin. Sie lächelt, gießt
  Ein schelmisch Blicken auf ihr Kind, das schließt
Verschämt die Wimper, unter dunkler Locke.

Und übermüthig schaut der Bursch herein:
  „Aha, das wird für meine Braut der Schleier!"
Still denkt die Mutter an des Vaters Frei'n,

Vor fünfzehn Jahren! an den Herzensschrein
  Pocht just das Neunte! — „Ach, die alte Leier!
Ich taufe noch! Der Kukuk hol' die Freier!"

THE WEAVER.

IN scarlet gown and blouse like lily-flower
  And flowing veil, a peasant woman tends
  The shuttle, darting like a mouse. She lends
To the long beam her little hand's full power

To spin a web from silken floss. One dower
  She has — her beauty. How she laughs and sends
  A roguish twinkle to her child, that bends
At every glance its shame-faced head the lower!

Her forward boy looks in, exclaiming low:
  "Aha, my bride shall wear that long veil of hers!"
The mother muses on her husband's vow

Just fifteen years ago: "The ninth child now —
  The old, old tale! — beneath my heart's shrine hovers.
I'll christen more. — The devil take the lovers!"

Diamantenschleifer.

Schon dreißig Jahr an einem Rad
　　In Blei senk' ich den Stein,
Bis er die feinsten Kanten hat
　　Und Feuergluth darein.

Das Feuer aus dem Erdenschlund,
　　Das Keiner nachgemacht;
Das Feuer, das im Augengrund,
　　Nur Lieb' und Haß entfacht.

Das blitzt mich so geheimnißvoll
　　Und so verlockend an,
Was lichtlos aus der Tiefe quoll;
　　Ich bin der Zaubrer dann,

Durch dessen Hand die Kaiserin
　　Erst strahlend reich geschmückt —
Das Reinste, hohe Herrscherin,
　　Aus Ruß und Staub gedrückt.

THE DIAMOND-POLISHER.

THESE thirty years upon a wheel
  I sink the stone in lead,
'Till finest cuts at last reveal
  The deep fire's golden-red!

Those flames from out the earth's abyss
  No one can imitate;
The flames, that beauty's eyelids kiss,
  Are fanned by love or hate.

Mysteriously on me, who hang
  Spell-bound, its colors shine;
For rayless from the earth it sprang;
  The magic art is mine

Through which the mistresses of thrones
  Are dazzlingly arrayed —
But, noble dames, the purest stones
  Of soot and dust are made!

Der Geigenmacher.

Mir träumte, daß die Engel
   Im Chor herniedergeschwebt
In meine kleine Werkstatt —
   Vor Glück hab' ich gebebt!

Sie nahmen die Geigen alle
   Herab, wie Blumen geschaart,
Begannen ein Tremulieren
   Wie Aeolsharfen zart.

Dann schwoll es bis zum Brausen,
   Zur Jubelsymphonie,
Und schluchzte Klagen dazwischen —
   So weinen Menschen nie!

Es war der Sphären Jauchzen,
   Es war der Welten Leid;
Und lächelnd spielten die Engel
   Wie Kinder im Strahlenkleid.

THE VIOLIN-MAKER.

I DREAMED a chorus of angels
  Came down one night to me
Within my little workshop —
  I trembled with ecstasy!

They took the violins to them,
  As children the flowers they find;
They began an æolian quaver
  As soft as the sound of the wind.

And then to a symphony swelling,
  To a burst of joy did it grow;
But between I heard a sobbing —
  Ah, never do men weep so!

The spheres were singing with triumph,
  The worlds were sobbing with woe;
The angels were laughing and playing
  Like children with raiment aglow.

Nun sollt Ihr mich betten und legen;

Mir wird der Sarg nicht schwer;

ı kann die Geigen nicht hören

Von Menschenhänden mehr!

Come, take me now to the graveyard;
  No longer the coffin I fear;
The violin-playing of mortals
  I never again can hear!

Steinschneider.

Wir sägen, sägen, sägen hin und her,
   Tagaus, tagein, jahrein, jahraus,
   In Sonnenbrand und Sturmgebraus,
   Und langsam steigt das Gotteshaus —
Wir sehen's nimmermehr!

Wir sägen, sägen, sägen her und hin.
   Die Sonne sticht, das Wasser zischt,
   Der Augen Kraft in Staub erlischt,
   Und unser Nam' in Staub verwischt —
Kein Ruhm und kein Gewinn!

Wir sägen, sägen, sägen immer noch!
   Du lieber Gott im Himmelblau,
   Siehst jeden Stein Du wohl genau,
   Die armen Leut' an Deinem Bau,
Die Niemand achtet doch?

THE STONE-CUTTER.

WE hammer, hammer, hammer on and on,
    Day-out, day-in, throughout the year,
  In blazing heat and tempests drear;
  God's house we slowly heavenward rear —
We'll never see it done!

We hammer, hammer, hammer, might and main.
  The sun torments, the rain-drops prick,
  Our eyes grow blind with dust so thick;
  Our name in dust, too, fadeth quick —
No glory and no gain!

We hammer, hammer, hammer ever on.
  O blessed God on Heaven's throne,
  Dost thou take care of every stone
  And leave the toiling poor alone.
Whom no one looks upon?